C. Liao

A JOY PROPOSED

A JOY PROPOSED

Poems
by T. H. White

WITH AN INTRODUCTION
AND AFTERWORD &
NOTES BY
Kurth Sprague

THE UNIVERSITY OF GEORGIA PRESS
ATHENS

ACKNOWLEDGMENTS

I am indebted to the Trustees of the Estate of T. H. White, and to David Higham Associates, White's agents, for permission to quote from the White Collection held in the Humanities Research Center at The University of Texas at Austin. I am grateful to the Humanities Research Center for making White's poetry, contained in so many disparate sources in the Collection, so readily available to me.

K. S.

CONTENTS

INTRODUCTION

In the fall of 1927 a group of T. H. White's Cambridge dons, upon learning that White was suffering from tuberculosis, raised a collection of £200 to send him to Italy for a year's convalescence. Told – possibly by his mother – that he had six months to live, White began work on two novels and negotiated a contract for a book of poetry. Only gradually must it have been borne in upon White that he was not going to die quite so soon, not die young in Italy like Shelley and Keats; indeed, it is likely that many of these early poems were penned in the belief that he laboured under sentence of death.

Upon his return to England and while he was in his last year at Cambridge, *Loved Helen and Other Poems* (London: Chatto & Windus, 1929) appeared with its Latin dedication to his mother, Constance White. Among White's papers is a letter dated 12 March 1929 which he wrote in Italian to a lady whom he had known in Positano. She had written White seeking Helen's identity. Addressing her as 'felicissima, gentilissima Signorina,' White answered her in romantic fashion:

> You asked who Helen is. *I don't know.* I seek her in the sky and on the sea every day but I cannot find her. Helen is as we say in English 'my better half' – (the superior half) – my only woman. We are very sure of not meeting.

The 'gentilissima Signorina' – astringent but herself disconcertingly romantic – would have none of White's posturing: she sent the letter back to White, with comment:

> You do not find her because you cannot love with that type of love which transforms and beautifies everything, makes us blindly believe that we have found our ideal. It is only when it starts vanishing or when it is no more within us that [love] makes us speak as you are speaking. Otherwise love would not exist for anybody.

It may be that these remarks about love are perceptive and just, but they demonstrate an insensitivity to the sincerity of White's romantic pose which, in his evident pleasure at having a created character taken for real, he adopted with such youthful relish. It may be that White never experienced the kind of incandescent, transforming love of which she speaks, but his poetry shows that he remained painfully aware of its possibility, that he

ix

quite probably desired its achievement above all else, and that he was supremely able to describe his plight. The 'gentilissima Signorina' ignores White's genuine concern that he might never find a Helen for his Paris. In fact, the search seems to have taken him the next thirty-one years, and when he found her he would be content to admire her from a distance.

The only child of a disastrous mating, White was born in Bombay in 1906. Constance White, whom White would limn in vitriol as the cruel Queen Morgause in *The Witch in the Wood*, was a thirty-year-old spinster when she married to spite her mother; she found herself aghast at the demands of sexual intimacy. She lavished attention on her son and then, withholding her affection, treated him with indifference. His father, Garrick White, from whom White inherited his interest in nature and love of animals, was an alcoholic of epic proportion who on at least one occasion had been known to climb into the mosquito-netted marriage bed with a lighted oil lamp in one hand, a loaded revolver in the other. Searing nursery memories stayed long with White: he was thirty-two and a successful author when he wrote 'Of Hapless Father'. At preparatory school and later at Cheltenham (he was four when he was taken to England), White endured corporal punishment: 'Dr Prisonface' is his passionate assessment of those years as well as of his first teaching post after graduation from Cambridge.

An absolute need to prove a love by hurting it and inviting hurt himself, and the contradictory desire compelling him to possess another soul and yet to abjure meddling were shown in the series of outrageous love affairs upon which White embarked from time to time, in which (if we are to take him at his word) he demonstrated an impressive ability to choose for the objects of his affection women whose ages (young, very young) or background (at least one barmaid) or both (an eighteen-year-old debutante) rendered them quite out of the question for serious consideration as wives.

During the ten-year period from the summer of 1936 when he resigned as Head of the English Department at Stowe in order to write full-time until his arrival on Alderney in the spring of 1946 in order to escape the high taxation on his earnings from *Mistress Masham's Repose*, White lived and wrote in remote locations. The five-shillings-a-week Victorian game-keeper's lodge on the Stowe estate; the eighteenth-century farmhouse, Doolistown, where he spent the war years, close to the fishing on the Boyne; Duke Mary's, the stone cottage in the Yorkshire dales lent him by his friend David Garnett: these were the rustic fastnesses from which White seldom ventured, save for supplies, on book-buying expeditions, for shooting or fishing trips, or for one of his self-destructive drinking bouts. It is only a partially satisfactory explanation of White's reclusiveness to say that it

x

stemmed from something medieval and monkish in his nature, or that his pacifist tendencies drove him out of England during the war years, or – more persuasive an answer perhaps – that these retreats were cheap, available, and generally in known neighbourhoods close to rural pursuits. The remainder of the explanation lies, I think, in the fact that White, so comfortable with the Early Fathers, and the inheritor of the old Indian Civil Service virtues, felt the need to preserve a limited vulnerability.

If this book has a distinctly Irish flavour, it is scarcely surprising, for thirty of these fifty-seven poems were written while White was in Ireland during the years 1939-1945, twenty-six of them composed in the fall of 1939, eleven during twelve days in September of that year. An infrequent host, White, temporarily in funds from the success of *Sword in the Stone*, had taken Sheskin Lodge in County Mayo for that month, and had seen his hopes for a gathering of his friends dashed by Hitler's invasion of Poland. He was left to finish his month's tenancy alone. Although White was rewriting *The Witch in the Wood* and outlining *The Ill-Made Knight*, his febrile teeming mind found little outlet in company or conversation. He was cut off from the company of his friends in England. Back at Doolistown, his daily conversation – meat and drink to a man of White's ferocious intellectual appetite – was curtailed to the unchallenging (and unchanging) topics which his well-meaning but unsophisticated landlords, the McDonaghs, felt comfortable discussing. His sole companion was his beloved red setter, Brownie. White's journals for those years, the testament of his hopes and fears, reflect his agony over the war and his place in it – ('It is better to make civilisation than to defend it,' runs one entry, bravely) – his growing preoccupation with nature and the animal world, his growing disaffection from mankind. It is in these journals that a great deal of White's finest poetry first appears.

In 1962, less than two years before his death, White commissioned a privately printed, limited edition (100 copies) of his poems. From a glance at the contents of this book, some of which had been written as early as 1938, one can see that *Loved Helen*'s poet, though present, is less obviously in evidence; instead, his figure is illumined by the description of his concerns. One of the most remarkable poems in the 1962 book is White's tribute 'For Julie Andrews'. *Camelot*'s Guenever, Miss Andrews cheered White's last years by involving him with *Camelot*'s out-of-town production in Boston in 1960, and by visits with her husband to White on Alderney. As an exemplar of dramatic skills she recommended herself to White, the connoisseur of enthusiasms. And she was young. White, vulnerable to the innocence of youth (his own included, as a look at 'To My Self, Forty Years Ago' will show), recast in her honour the first stanza of 'Paris' but instead of finishing off the poem with 'I am that curst Paris,' he adds a new verse:

Julie, the thousand prows aimed at her heart,
The tragic Queen, comedian and clown,
Keeps Troy together, not apart,
Nor lets one tower fall down.

Loved Helen's youthful poet, who saw Helen as 'my only woman,' and who was 'very sure of not meeting' her, has been replaced by an aging poet content, at distance, to list a lady's virtues. Yet both voices, the swanking romantic and the firebanked greybeard, are White's utterly, are both sincere.

Above all else in writing, White prized sincerity of heart. As one of his students from Stowe would recall, what mattered 'was what you *felt*, and whether your feelings were genuine, personal and sincere; and what was despicable was to serve up stock responses or clever aphorisms or second-hand opinions.' White stayed constant to this ideal. Copied in French on the endpapers of his copy of I. A. Richards's *Principles of Literary Criticism* is this passage from André Gide's *Les Faux-Monnayeurs*:

Sincerity! When I speak of it, I think only of . . . sincerity. If I turn
to myself, I cease to understand what the word means, I am only
what I believe I am – and that fluctuates constantly, so that often, if
I were not there to bring them together, my morning self would not
recognize my evening self.

In his poems, White's morning's and evening's selves cry out to us from his every age, from his every condition: rash youth pretending, middle age reflecting, maturity appraising; the antiquary contemplating, the countryman observing, the falconer lamenting, the naturalist discoursing, the pacifist inveighing; the writer recording. Their voices arouse resonance with the voices of those whom White much admired: Auden, Housman, Hardy, Hopkins, Kipling, Swinburne and Shakespeare. White's sincerity was sincerity of heart as well as of posture, and he was no more at ease in aping the fashions of modern-day poetry than he was in incorporating the notions of modern-day morality into *The Once and Future King*.

It comes as a surprise that these poems, so steadfastly traditional in their shape and feeling, should have been written during a time so resolutely iconoclastic in matters poetic. But White eschewed the merely iconoclastic. In his copy of Richards, he has scored this passage:

> There is no more 'a proper place' for sound and sense in poetry than there is one and only one 'proper shape' for an animal. A dog is not a defective cat, nor is Swinburne a defective kind of Hardy.

White's tiny, elegant handwriting fills nearly the whole of the margin:

> Children enjoy sweets (Swinburne) and grown people may feel benefited by gin & tonic (shall we say Hardy?) but it can still be said that the best thing to put into our mouths – judged by the standards of continuing to live efficiently – is a good wholesome meal which includes soup & fish & meat & sweets & savoury *and* gin & tonic. So there is a 'proper' kind of meal, and Shakespeare is *better* than Swinburne. Here is a Roland in nutrition-analogy for Richards's Oliver of a cat's home.

As readers of this book will learn to their delight, there is indeed a banquet in these pages, with every kind of course for every palate. I can do no better than to recall David Garnett's words in his review of *They Winter Abroad*: 'The wit, the brilliance! Come . . . come, gather and fall shamelessly on the feast!'

Kurth Sprague

Austin, Texas
June, 1979

A JOY PROPOSED

PARIS

Helen whose face was fatal must have wept
Many salt tears to keep her eyes so bright
Many long nights alone: and every night
Men died, she cried, and happy Paris kept
Sweet Helen.

I am that curst Paris.

LOST

Be kind, Helen, I am so tired of thinking;
There are so many difficult corridors of thought,
With equal iron banisters leading back again:
So many stone stairs, Helen, up which I sought
To rediscover the windy sky, and stand, blinking,
In the lost sunlight: as bright as pain,
Helen. I would give almost anything now
Even for pain. If one day down my iron avenues
The tubes and cubes, leading, at last, me right,
Should lose their remorseless patterns and diffuse
Into a kinder symmetry, and show me how
After a white hand pointing Exit, shine the stars at night:
Should I, appreciating the right gesture, fall dead?
I should walk out quietly and stand still
With the air in my hair and my feet in the wet dew,
Eternally motionless, without want, or will,
Not proud any more, Helen, of this poor head:
And I daresay even that's not true.

COLD

The colourless world the moon made, made me think
Of that vast spacially and temporally different time
Of steel grey shadow and rime
When from the bowelled earth
Futural man, having resought his birth,
Shall rise to re-explore from the bright caverns he has yet to sink.
The dying sun then made a moon, whose light
Reflects no sun but only the thin stars' cold metal
Which burns the hand, will show no leaf or petal,
No grass on ground too hard for covering against the night,
No twig for birds to settle:
Or if half petrified twigs frosted and darked to iron
No birds to settle on them.
Only perhaps silurian snakes will find some moss to lie on,
Their own slow blood cold enough, and their eyes blind enough,
To bear the unbearable pain of ice and weight of dusk upon them:
Moving a mile in fifty years,
Eating at a grey silver midday once a century.
And he who peers
Through the eternal mist at a new old horizon
Stranger than mystery
Since finite and yet impossible, too still, too lost, too old,
Will know what I felt on this October evening,
   the meaning of stone-cold.

I've been a bitter friend to you,
And you to me.
It was a bitter hour that bore us two,
And a black day, my dearest love, that brought us through
So many miles of land and sea;
Through more than twenty years of different days,
Through time and space,
Through severance to be
Never more severed.
Oh, you'll not forget me. Our two ways
May break apart and stormily retrace
The miles of land and sea and years and time and space
That our two lines unconsciously endeavoured
Towards meeting, back from meeting.
But, my hard heart, my bitter sweeting,
This was no moon affair; we have shed no tears,
And no, you'll not forget me;
Not in forty years.

DR PRISONFACE

This pretty boy, mischievous, chaste, and stupid,
With bouncing bum and eyes of teasing fire,
This budding atom, happy heart, young Cupid,
Will grow to know desire.

Anxious Mamma, discern the signs of rapture,
Observe his sensuous wriggles in the bath.
His plump brown legs design their future capture,
Their virgin quelled, their tenderness and wrath.

Happy immoral imp, if this continues
He will, no doubt, grow up a shameless sensualist.
He won't despise his genitals and sinews,
Won't know that it is 'beastly' to be kissed.

Stuff him in Etons quick, and send him packing
To Dr Prisonface his breezy school.
That old rheumatic man with threats and whacking
Will justly bring this body to the rule.

Send your bright dreaming angel then to Dr Prisonface
So that he may be taught his 'beastly' loins to rule,
So that he may be learned what is and isn't cricket,
So that he may be a product of the good old school.

His legs are beautiful but he must hate them,
Starve them till sterile and when past their prime
He may be allowed to marry somebody exactly like him
And have a jolly good time.

Till then, for you can't quite kill his angel,
He'll fall at intervals and take a whore,
Shamefully take her in the night time and afterwards hate himself
All the more, and do it the more.

He will convey the blight to his own marriage bed
Which will exactly resemble Dr Prisonface's:
Surreptitiously wrestling with his wife in the darkness,
Putting her with averted eyes through hasty shameful paces.

(7)

Dark and remorseful and dirty will be his copulation,
In Dr Prisonface's hell, among the wicked.
But never mind, he'll be a credit to the nation;
And we all hope, we all so hope, he will be good at cricket.

OF HAPLESS FATHER

Of hapless father hapless son
My birth was brutally begun,
And all my childhood o'er the pram
The father and the maniac dam
Struggled and leaned to pierce the knife
Into each other's bitter life.
Thus bred without security
Whom dared I love, whom did not flee?

Well blest! Now, in ten million sighs,
One can stand on without surprise.

LOOKING AT THE SKULL OF
ST ANDREW ON THE ALTAR AT AMALFI

This skull is the deserted egg of an extinct species,
Bleached, blown, and long past being stale or rotten,
A mineral remnant, one of the collector's pieces
In which the Dodo of the mind was once begotten.

I feel my own skull, through its warm and mobile coating
Of quick, comfortable hair and the neck's firm flesh,
Nestling in rosy enclosure, cushioned and cradled, floating
In the fruit's womb, a nutty kernel, a fledgling fresh.

How smoothly it articulates upon its nervous column,
Nourished with scarlet sap in the rich autumn!
How fruitfully it sniffs up balmy aromas through its five
   living issues,
Warm and ripening in its cradle of juicy tissues!

Strange but natural that my cosy kernel –
Its flesh fermented – must later bleach alone,
A fruit no longer, but self-sufficient: an eternal,
Hard-shrivelled, clean-nibbled, pleasant, peachless stone.

READING GIRALDUS CAMBRENSIS

Look at the peace of inanimate things,
The sanity of stones,
The probity of pasture fields, dead trees,
Old hills and patient bones.

Giraldus tells us that the Archbishop stood
To preach at Parc-y-Cappel
'On a verdant plain' – wherefore the people
Built there a chapel.

This bishop in eleven eighty-eight
Preached them the Third Crusade.
(A footnote adds that 'Chapel Field' now marks
The sermon that he made.)

Think, when at Parc-y-Cappel, what young Taffy
Here took the Cross.
Did he sing, marching Europe, sad Welsh hymns
And look at a loss?

Think of that stream of miserable men,
The half not knowing
Where, with their mormals, rags and wretched staffs,
They were meekly going.

Think of the Sickness of the Hoste, the famine,
The ant-like army's woe,
Betrayed by leaders, knackered by black Arabs,
Eight hundred years ago.

The sorrow-serpent wound by that Archbishop
Has wound away its pain:
But Chapel Field, now churchless, is once more
A verdant plain.

Look at the peace of inanimate things,
The sanity of stones,
The probity of pasture fields, dead trees,
Old hills and patient bones.

READING FRIAR CLYNN

Friar Clynn the annalist,
making ready to die
of the Black Death in 1348,
closed his annals as follows:

'Videns haec multa mala et mundum
totum quasi in maligno positum, inter
mortuos mortem expectans donec
veniat, sicut veraciter audivi et
examinivi sic in scripturam redegi,
et ne scriptura cum scriptore pereat
et opus simul cum operario
deficiat, dimitto pergamenam pro
opere continuando, si forte
in futuro homo superstes remaneat,
an aliquis de genere Adae hanc
pestilenciam possit evadere et
opus continuare inceptam.'

To the unborn, if births there be,
Who take man's Nature after me,
This message from antiquity:

Written amid man's sorrow and dread,
Expecting death among the dead,

The sky unbirded but by bombs,
The earth crawled over with iron tombs,
The armies creeping under the earth,
The fruits of humus rotting at birth,
The little germs of future diseases
Gnawing at tissues as them pleases,
The gastric juices of the poor men
Teasing out bellies, the acids biting,
The minds suffocating and shame on the pen,
And all, all madly lying and fighting:
O man unborn, listen to our woe,
O man, unborn, who must learn or go.

(13)

First, don't think we were savager than you.
We thought so of our ancestors too.
But the heart of man will never be tame,
It will always have one quarter of shame,
The scissors will come for you just the same.

Secondly, know that the reason for war
Is Natural Property, now as before.
My empire, colony, country, or place
Are the certain seasons of death and disgrace.
But abolish my Property, and you'll find
That it comes back the same, or in similar kind.

Thirdly, don't think that life is for pleasure.
Happiness is only half the measure.
So, if you live with Joy as a lord,
It will turn to woe of its own accord.
Seek to be happy, or to be at peace,
And you will have sorrow, and war will increase.
Give gifts for return: they will meet with short shrift.
Peace for peace, not for you, and the gift for the gift.

Fourthly and finally, don't suppose
That it matters whether Man stays or goes.
Don't think that Man is the centre of things,
The lord of the legs and the fins and the wings.
Not a star will blink if he goes out tomorrow.
Not a sand in this sand dune feels his sorrow.
Not a sod of the earth but forgets his furrow.
Not a rat will regret him, nor rabbit in burrow
Browse less beautifully because he is below.

ENDURANCE VILE ✝

When I look at your comely head
And the long fingers delicately live
And the bright life born to be dead
And the happy blood to be shed
And the eagerness that can not survive
And the trust made to be betrayed
And the hope certain to be cheated cold
And the young joy to age and fade
And the making to be unmade
And even the endurance to grow old,

I die within me. And I curse
The witless fate of man without all cure.
Music I curse, and verse,
And beauty worse,
And every thing that helps us to endure.

A CHOIR BOY SINGING

Full heart, too much
Too full to touch,
On brim to spill,
Pour clear, flow still.

Know not, but sigh.
Think not, but die.
Hope not, but high
Ache against ill.

Sing, but unwarned.
Strive, but unarmed.
Though doomed, yet trust.
As yet unharmed,
Woo the wan dust.

LE COMMUN ADVENEMENT

Nostradamus

Strange birds will cry in the air, 'Today, Today!'
Serpents will raise their multiple arms in the sea.
Earth endways will edge and all beasts there be
Wail with one woe of a wail as it passes away.

And it, aureate, awful, billowing free,
Pinkly pervading and blazing and dimming the dun sun's ray
Will with a whoosh begone with us on, for ever and all and a day,
Beridding itself with a rapturous rush of them and of you and of me.

ALL SAINTS' DAY

This morning's Mass was made by the Church Militant.
It was here the holiday of All Hallowes.
Our broken battalions beaten,
Our companies compassed with crime,
The shattered soldiery stood.
We formed square, outfacing the conquering foe.
We drew the rest of our rags around us.
We stood straight to the worn-out weapons, at bay.
And here, in the dust of defeat and the darkness,
Surrounded by sorrows and vanquished by sins –
All fresh and full-fed and outranging our arms –
We, the outworn, the outmatched, the outnumbered,
Raised our eyes to the Saints who were safe – and we cheered.

They had comfort, were carefree, and could have cheered us
From their nest in the nimbus. But no,
It was we, the abandoned, the bitter, the beaten,
The fighting defeated, unsolaced by Mother or Infant,
Who raised a proud cheer – for the Church which had
                           once been Triumphant.

A JOY PROPOSED

Omne animal, says the Roman bard,
Post coitum triste. Yes, it is hard
That we should have to do what leaves us marred.
The fervent maniac falters on his prey,
Droops back foredone, his animal drained away.
I was a beast before, good thing to be,
But now I am spirit only, mental me.
All sorrow is on the relict, not through sin.
It is because he had two parts within –
One part the happy Beast, whom loving killed,
The other Mind, who lives alone, unspilled,
Holy and horrible, abstract and apart,
Absolute, agonized and pure of heart.
Mind now persists, his partner being dead.
The ever sorrowful Mind is in my bed.

That bard was wrong to make all animals sad.
Only Man suffers it. The Beasts are glad.
They die all at once, being perfect wholes,
To rise again as animals, not souls.
I wonder what tricked Man to evolute
From the sweet singleness he had as Brute
And boast of this same Mind: his dead-sea fruit.

ON FALLING
IN LOVE AGAIN AFTER SEVEN YEARS

'These living bodies that we wear
So change by every seventh year
That in a new dress we appear.'
        – Andrew Young.

In seven years this aching nude
Has all its particles renewed.
Each organ, sinew, bit of bone,
Now turned to stone, now turned to stone,
Will grow again and from within
Refill a new, forgetful skin.
The ache will go, the woe be done,
In time to meet another one.

Medusa One, Medusa Two,
Well, I have done with both of you,
And must, with seven years' slow pain,
Re-grow the tissues once again.
The heart, now stony-broke, will mend
And seek in time a final friend,
And she, who shall be all to me,
Shall be addressed: Medusa Three.

But when Medusa Three departs
What way can men re-grow their hearts?
Unresilient, defeated,
Hopeless and puzzled, old and cheated,
No seven years left in which to slough
The skin and make another Now?
Then will come Medusa Four.
Into her Grave my heart will pour.

MY JACK-MERLIN, BALAN

Died of Heart Failure

When I was little I was led captive by strangers, and taught
   by a stranger.
I was motherless and fatherless and my folk were far.
I held my head upright as betokened my lineage
And bore the barbarian as I was born to bear.
I fled never and went forward and was fearless,
First to learn, friendly, following what I was for.
By the waters of Babylon I was bold, leading captivity captive:
My feathers were fleet and my brown eye clear.
When Man ago came to us, foodbringer for childhood,
I first flew down and advanced for his cheer.
I, confident also when the Dark Stranger mantled over me,
Advanced into natural death as the falcon comes to the lure.
Death was my first and only natural piece of Nature.
Death was as further as birth, and I went without fear.
I fell over sideways, I laid down the head which ever slept
   upright.
I went forward then also, to learn under the dark wings, and
   be there.

LINES CUT
ON THE COTTAGE WINDOW

A bitter heart lay here and yet
It was not bitter to the bone.
It made what Time does not unmake
All hopeful, and alone.

STARS AND MOUNTAINS

I was alone for dinner, with one candle,
Reading a book propped against it, about the stars.
There was a grouse and wine and outside the French window
Nephin waited for Mars.

The Romans were never in Erin. Their plethoric bird,
The pheasant who falls to the pop of the English earl,
Is a rarity with us. His clutter seldom is heard.
But in our best room, in a bower of mother of pearl
Printed 'Present from Cork', and of pampas grass placed in pink pots,
Proudly upon the piano the pheasant is seen.
He is perched on a boulder of papier-mâché done green.
He is spurred, he is plumed, he is dusty, and gorgeously rots.
He stretches his tail to the moths and his orgulous bosom though dead
To the paraffin lamp. He wobbles a little if I
Tread on the loose board. He does not remember the sky.
The person who stuffed him has given him horns on his head,
Like the Long-eared Owl, and I also, I do not remember
Whether he had horns or not – as he flew and he floated on high,
Dustless, displaying and dreading to die,
Grand in his gold mail, a living, a light-giving ember
Refulgent from the red wood to this undreamed of rath on the piano
Some long-ago December.

THE GAME-KEEPER

Stopping suddenly by a bog-hole, half in, to pluck
A reddish root of little distinction from the muck
With his gentle fingers, Joyce said: 'Here is a small
Carnivorous plant.' Between the soft ball
Of one kind thumb and finger he held it out
Without much certainty and without
Pride.
He implied
That we had probably seen it before, and we
Would know many things more curious, and it
Was only of the bog. But we could see
The small flies it had overcurled and every bit
Was a miracle of kind. Joyce had yearly known
More than was in all our hearts, and this was all his own.

BOO TO A HERON

Crane we call her in Erin, the creature,
But in Hampshire: heron, or – shortly – harn.
She rows over the red bog in airy innocence
Waving her wan wings in wild timidity
Sweeping her shadow with spoon-shaped plume.
Nooked is her neck as she floats along Nephin
Cradling the cool bill on her calm bosom
In search of some small fish in our sweet streams.
Finding a fishing ground she furls up her feathers,
Thrusts out her thin legs and thumps on the ground.
There, in the deep tunnel dug by the turf drain,
She hoves with her grey hackles harried by the wind.
There in the teeming burn, tired and untidy,
She listens and lingers with her lemon eye.

The boys of Bellacorick are bitter to Miss Mollern.
They are ware of a weakness which is her distress.
Such is her sensibility, she is subject to the vapours
And on her affliction they tyrannously trade.
The mannikins of Mayo, when they mark down a crane,
Crawl along craftily and come to her drain.
Then they leap up lustily, loud crying 'Hoo!'
Whirling their wild arms in wicked fun,
Bellowing like banshees, 'Bellacorick Aboo!'
Which causes faint Mollern to flop down foredone.

CURLEWS

Cur-lee, Cur-lew, a plaintive jew
Of barry plume and Hebrew beak,
With angled elbow on the wind
He partly circles where I seek.

Allusive circle! Wanderer,
Iscariot if so you be,
Trust if you can one gentile heart,
No pogrom fear at least from me.

They burn your bog, my fellow men,
In spring when eggs point-inward lie.
Well may you hove beyond our range
And well Cur-lew, Cur-lee may cry.

Poor bird! Your unemphatic curve,
Your vague, disturbed, evasive turn
Alluded, I know, to what I seek:
A centre they have failed to burn.

There, at that centre – where I stand,
In patience poring on the ground –
Will lie one thing of two I love:
The hint your music circles round.

Either the mother and the wife,
Stock still six inches from my toe,
Sits close, beak straight, with button eye,
Rigid with fear, but still won't go.

Or else, still warm, in shallow scoop,
Four khaki eggs of mottle green
Are parked like tanks in camouflage,
By my reconnaissance not seen.

(27)

I stand, I focus, change the lens
Within my living eye and hope,
Until the object, under nose,
Leaps like the clicked kaleidoscope.

Bright eye, speckled feather, Rabbi beak,
Stay still for all there's harm in me.
God bless the work and may four more
Fly round to sing Cur-lew, Cur-lee.

THE COW

It was All Saints' Day, first Mass, then dinner;
I, with good food inside me, went out to piss.
The radio, merry of music; and calories; and gin a
Heartier glow had given us than I can say in this.
'For all the Saints' they sang, and I in mirth
Sang as I piddled of the saints in bliss.
The green earth rang to my water, while, over a wall,
The deep eyes of the halt cow wondered me, and saints, and all.

A YOUNG COCK GROUSE

This sooty grouse – yet tawny and touched with red –
Weighs handsome on my hand, although he's dead.
One wing reflects the sky. A steely light
Gleams from the primaries he oiled last night,
The twelve swift swords with which he hewed his flight.
His crop of heather, which my falcon split
Footing him, spills on my hand. Each bit
Is cleaner than cook's salad, fresh and green,
With lilac buds surprising to be seen.
Such was his simple craft, to snip all day and seek
His livelihood of leaves with agricultural beak.

Joyce says, 'An old cock.' But some tint I see,
Remembering me of youth. I disagree:
'I think he's this year's bird.' Joyce takes him, dumb,
Opens the bleeding beak, inserts a thumb,
And weighs him by the lower jaw – which breaks.
'Quite right. This year's.' 'Why so?' 'Well, sir, it takes
An old bird to stand this. He's got more pate.
A young bird's beak will break with his own weight.'

How did Man find this out? Who first took heart
To lift his grouse by that unlikely part
And go on lifting till he learned the art?
Seeing how stupid Man is, it's unnerving
To think how long he must have been observing.

LETTER FROM A GOOSE-SHOOTER

On Inniskea, long before Patrick came,
Stood the stone idol of the secret name:
The magic people made him. No surprise,
No threat, no question lit his two round eyes,
Nor had he other features. Consciousness
Was all his feeling, all his creed 'I wis.'
He watched the wild geese twenty centuries.

Inniskea is an island. Ten years gone
The human race lived here, the windows shone
With candles over the water, and men
Fished currachs, women wellwards went from ben.
There was a King to rule the island then,
Chosen for might, who had his Admiral
Of All the Inniskeas. The priest's sick call
Was this cold pasture's only festival.

Mass was so far off, with such storms between,
And in the dark nights moved so much unseen
On the wild waters, that Man's beating heart
Still sometimes turned towards the old God's art.
Much magic was made with the dew. The wells
Secretly stirred with strange internal spells.

To keep the Agent off, or the Excise,
Fires were lit before the God of Eyes
And dances made around his stone, sunwise.
Their old cold Godstone they, for comfort, dressed
In one new suit each year: his Sunday best.

Then the remorseless sea, the all-beleaguering,
The crafty, long-combed sea, the stark and whistling,
The savage, ancient sea, master at waiting,
Struck once.
        Two hours later the Mainland
Received one man, a saucepan in his hand,
Astride an upturned currach. At the Inn

They gave him clothes without, whisky within,
Such as they could: but he nor left nor right
Altered his eyes. Only with all his might,
This man bailed with his saucepan all that night.
In half one hour of squall, from calm to calm, the Main
Holding his ten mates drowned had fallen on asleep again.

Nobody painted the houses after.
The islanders lost all heart for laughter.
Work was a weariness, dances were done,
On the island whose pride of Man was gone.

Now I am all alone on Inniskea,
All alone with the wind and with the sea.
The corrugated iron, rusted brown,
Gives a burnt look to the abandoned town.
The roofs are ruins and the walls are down.

The Land Commission took the people ashore.
King Phillip Lavell is here no more.
They have even taken away the God Who Saw,
To stand in Dublin Museum. From ten till four
He eyes the opposite wall.
                              Oh, God of Eyes,
Bound there in darkness and deprived of skies,
Know that your Geese are back. Know that their cries
Lag on the loud wind as, by candlelight,
At Inniskea's one fire I, your last subject, write:
Lulled by their laughter, cradled in their night.

WILD GEESE

You two lying there, you two at my feet,
Dark, done-for dummies on the darker peat,
I did you in, I made you into meat.

Almost human, the geese are, wild and free,
Sagacious, sociable, no harm to me.
Before Man was you were, and since he is
He has not learned half your democracies.
You mastered speech, your strange and nasal tongue,
Most rich in sagas, when the Apes were young.
In forty years of flight, my clan has turned,
Like curdled milk, the air by you long learned.
Our aircraft rule the sky I've raped you from,
Which you ruled twenty million years without one bomb.
Almost human? No, no. *De mortuis.*
Humans have far to go before they are geese.

But it is the wild cry falling out of the night.
It is the wave of black wings on a crack of light.
It is the wandering wedge upon the height.
Is it because to Man flight is a lie?
Does my base metal hate to see you high?
It was your smoke-line pibroch of the sky
Which was too beautiful as you passed by:
It was because I loved you that you had to die.

SHESKIN

Sheskin, the music of your name and your waters
That night when there was an inch and a half in the rain gauge
And all night all round the lodge and from the spouts of the verandah
You chuckled: we were waiting for a flood.
Sheskin, your lovely lonely tunnels of rhododendrons,
And absurd monkey puzzles and riot of vegetable vigour,
And the dragon blood of the fuchsias in forests, and primroses
And peas in September: all this in twenty miles of bog.
Sheskin, your grouse whose crops startled me, spilling sweet heather
Under the falcon's foot and blood-spotted train, and sea-trout
With tiger fins, and red salmon who would not take
Even with all our prayers: leaping, leaping out of the Owenmore.
Sheskin, oh Sheskin, all this and all the things that are Sheskin,
As beautiful as infinity: please let me come back to you in peace.
Please be there, and let me be there to come back,
Back to our secret stream which harps into the deep basin
Under the old kiln where they used to dry malt for potheen.
That ice-clear summer stream of music fizzing with bubbles,
Sliding over the flat slabs to the little waterfall,
Is you, Sheskin; is me, Sheskin; oh, Nephin and Slieve Car be true.

GOODBYE NOW

Well then, as we say in Ireland: 'Goodbye, now.'
We don't say 'God be with you, and Mary too' (or few of us).
Only Goodbye Now: and the Now means,
Oh, Sheskin, it means all of my heart's love and how
I will be back soon, please God, to your free scenes.
It means the heart-in-the-handshake and burdheachas
Le dia for Nephin and Slieve Car, and, too,
It means, dear soul, that blood in this cold heart
Will always have some bog water in it and will
Suddenly stand still
At the smell of turf or sight of mountain view,
Or a grouse wing flicking dark against the hill,
Crying Sheskin, crying with the salmon leap: I start!
Sheskin, be true. Be true.

WHEN DYNASTIES ARE DEAD

When dynasties are dead, as die they must;
When sorrow is silent, and red swords are rust;
When man is a memory, and his dreadful dreams are dust,
I am Carslieve. Nephin and I keep trust:
True to the untrue, to the unjust just.

DOGS HAVE NO SOULS

A Memoir of My Setter Brownie

*The old Irish greeting used to be: 'God save all here,
barrin' the dog and the cat.' This was a correct wish,
according to the doctrine that animals have no souls.*

Love throws a reticence about our lives.
Men seldom write the memoirs of their wives.
But, tender nose, to whom these words are only
A texture of kind noise, I would be lonely
If you should die tonight – lonely in having
No picture or poem to tell our loving.
Also, these Powers of theirs who feed on heart
Laid their foul ambush for us from the start.
Dogs must still die, men live, and we must part.
So, like a thrifty banker, I lay by
My store of Brownie, for the day you die.

This store contains a nose pushed under mine
To make me stop when reading. It contains
A loud hurrah for Walk or Mice or Gun,
Your simple alphabet and sum of brains.
It has a sharp-nailed paw to hurt my hand
If I forget or do not understand.
But there . . . this catalogue will do no better
Than to describe us any kind of setter.

Well then, one picture to preserve the tint
Of my slave mistress with her sweet heart in it:
Today I shot a mallard which fell down
Across the Boyne, and thus my darling Brown:
First, at the bang, much leaping, then a stand,
Seeing him up-so-down so far from land;
Realization next, and memory drops
A hint that ducks taste oily on the chops –
Repulsive birds, and to retrieve from water
Is hardly work for a red setter's daughter.

(37)

Quick then, forestalling the unjust request,
Brown hurries off elsewhere to do her best,
And seeks him soundly in the opposite
Direction, in some reeds, with busy wit.
'Come, come,' I say. 'A truce to this deceit.
Go fetch yon bird, and lay him at my feet.'
'Dear master,' saith she. 'What a charming day!
Do you not think it would be best to play,
As thus, at Mice, beneath yon temperate sky?'
She tempts me with shy barks and bashful eye,
Seeking to charm, to please, divert the mind
And soothe her master lest he prove unkind.

'Enough, hysteric! You perceive your duty.
No inhibitions, now. Fetch him, my beauty.'
At this, the stern though kindly tone of cheer,
She droops her quarters, fearing she must fear,
And looking on me closely says, 'Oh, dear!'
Long, long ago – forgive it, love – I would
Have beat, for what you had not understood,
Or could not do because of my dull teaching.
But now I say, 'Ah, well, my gentle sweeting,
You need the psycho-analyst, not beating.
We shan't fall out about such trash, my chuck.
Come, let's go home and leave the bloody duck.'

But listen to this, bitch, and you grim Powers.
When these two wait to pass the gatehouse towers,
My bitch goes with me. When I come to die,
We go together in love, my bitch and I.
Or, if you fear to let such love return,
Go to, and shut your gates. Sweeter to burn.

OFF TO THE WARS

To Brownie

Brownie, my Brownie, now that I am going –
This may be no good poem but it will be truth –
You have been to me mother and daughter,
Decency, kindness, love, beauty and youth.
Forget me then. Oh, forget me utterly.
Forget quick and be happy and live long.
If you remember for a minute, I shall die in badness,
Or live in ashes and beastly, remorseful, wrong.
Live you, tail flirting, eyes pleading,
In pleasure, in brownness, in trust of my race.
Only thus I shall live or die, my darling,
Not in disgrace.

BROWNIE, I AM FREE OF YOU

Brownie, I am free of you,
Who ruled my heart for 14 years!
O Freedom, all begun anew,
O iceblock heart, O tears!

My gentleness, my trustfulness,
My looker-up, my life,
My coward who leaned on my care
In vain, my child and wife,

My mother with the golden pelt,
Myself with melting eye,
My Brownie, rooted in the core,
My hoping lover-lie.

LOVE IS BLIND

God is love, the parson whined.
Yes, and is he also blind?

ALL FOR LOVE

God is love, the bishops tell.
Yes, I know. But love is hell.

NO TROUBLE

Thank God for the aged
And for Age itself, and Illness, and the Grave.
When you are old and ill, and particularly in the coffin,
It is no trouble to behave.

DETACHMENT

Say to this lady, 'I consider the question of
                              corporal punishment
Completely bewildering.'

And she will immediately answer: 'How dare you suggest
That I beat my children!'

THESE ARE THE EASY VERSES

These are the easy verses, which anybody can write
    in a minute:
So easy that more than two or three at a time
    Leave a taste in the mouth,
But oh my God
    If I could once get from my heart
    What is in it
About man and madness,
    Ambition and the blood of boys –

HIGH TIME

It is time to begin thinking what we shall write
On the war memorials; time to begin thinking
In what terms we shall describe our brothers as devils;
Time to begin inventing atrocity-stories and new bombs.
It is time to begin planning for the pestilence afterwards,
For the revolutions and the unbridled hates of the heart.
It is time to begin writing the songs of sentiment
Which are to be sung by the dying boys.

THE SCHOOLMASTER'S SONG

This boy was born
When I was a young man.
He came squealing and puckered, mauvish,
And was loved, when
I was all balled up with dreams and postures
And the gold haze in
My eyes, young too then, but feeling Methuselah to him.
And he grew and he tried and he touched and he eyed
And he went on
And all gathered round to protect
The young sun.

He paid for their love with his trust
And so waxed, and began
School boy, me than master of many:
Ink blotted, chewed pen,
Held up hand to leave room,
Gave grin for grin:
With milk teeth, candid eye, love for love. I
Was depended upon
And trusted by him till his schooling
Was over, and over his fun.

And now they have killed him.
But why did he scan
Latin verses, learn French, Pouvoir, pu?
Why the troublesome pen?
Why, when the slow pains that we took
To help him begin?
What for the protection he trusted, that failed him?
Why is he gone,
Born after, dead before, all wasted our love?
Why was this done?

We must not forget that Now is a moveable feast.
There was a Now once when hearts were heavy in Sparta
And many men of many empires have feared, and laughter
Has died on lips that are now skulls. But they were released.
Think of all those black Nows of the human pain
And the mad and merciless who made them.
Napoleon made heavy hearts, but Time unweighed them,
And Wars of Roses and Royalists have sunk into peace again.
There must have been lovers under Cromwell who thought,
All at an end! Must have been poets who could not see
    beyond Bosworth Field.
Well then. They are History now. Please God, we too may be taught
As History in another Now – all safe, secret and sealed.

A TRAIN

The cartridges will go before the coals:
Trains are not fragile, and coal will dig.
But then, as the dead mind closes down,
And the plague eats little and big,
And the electric and the h. & c. desert the town,
Then the trains too will be without coals.

Or if some lusus naturae of a train,
Having found coal and water somewhere, and a man
Who understands them, should perhaps chug
One startling day over the weedy metals which will span
The brambly counties, if not first dug
Up for munitions, it will be a train

At which we, in our homespun stare,
Nervously grasping our museum swords and rusty blades,
Wondering what new danger has outsprung
This old rattler from the lonely shades.
And we shall stand groping in the brain for memories young,
As the broken, rust-red chuff-chuff moles from our stare.

NAPOLEON CROWNED HIMSELF

Nobody ever offered me a crown,
   nor would it be very useful if I had it.
If it were a valuable crown you could sell it
And convert the money
   into something you wanted, I suppose.
But the mitred crown of the Holy Roman Empire,
And the crown of the thistle and the rose,
And the Pope's triple crown, and Caesar's of laurel,
And the poet's of bay, and all the other crowns
   of every jewel and temper,
If they were all worn one on top of the other even,
   would not be worth the quarrel.
The Emperor of the World, eating out of one crown
   and drinking from another,
And pissing in a third, and using a fourth
   for a bedpan for all I ken:
No, brother.
He would have bought at a loss
   if he bought with the blood of one dead man.

TIME FAST AND TIME SLOW

I can remember a time when spring and summer
Fled on so sweet and soft a wing
That, stretching my hand in winter,
Remained in the palm, for all looking, no thing.
The loveliness of leaves passed all thinking.
The sun on the skin was so shining.
The blood in that boy was bright becoming,
But fast fled and fared our lovely leafing.

Now Time is turned traitor to my spring and summer.
No heavy wing carries away the bitter minute.
I dread the century of a second now, dread and doubt
The agelong worlds of war and winter and weariness in it.

AN OUTMODED SONNET

Minds of less madness in more rural days
Who wrote by candles, went on foot, built strong;
Milton in grey, threading a gracious maze
Of linkèd sweetness; Herbert in full song;
And the unthinkable Shakespeare: men whose minds
With the old tools laid our foundations down,
Durably building for the imagined town –
The Unmean City – lovers of the spell which binds:

Surely in your day there was pain and fear
As deep as ours, as pitiful and bewildering?
Surely you grieved the grief which we feel here,
Tasting the blood of truth and innocent children?
Come then with dignity and help put on it
The old stiff dress of the outmoded sonnet.

PALOMIDES TO LA BEALE ISOUD

Hon. Madam! Kind regards! Immortal life
Be yours henceforth from 18th ultimo,
Is prayer which Palomides sings to fife
And tabor twice per diem. May you know
Ten thousand offspring (male) legitimate,
Each one well blessed with twenty thousand wives!
May each and all achieve whate'er he strives
With L. S. D., (D. V.), and godly fate.
May God Almighty, whom you much resemble,
Send cows and elephants to crowd your bed,
Waving their lofty trunks which squirm and tremble
To shade from sol your most respected head.
Kind Madam, Grand-Pa of this humble fish,
Calicut (failed) B. A., accept this wish.

THE ORDEAL HYMN

Life is blood, shed and offered;
   The eagle's eye can face this dree.
To beasts of chase the lie is proffered:
   Timor Mortis Conturbat Me.

The beast of foot sings Holdfast only,
   For flesh is bruckle and foot is slee.
Strength to the strong and the lordly and lonely.
   Timor Mortis Exultant Me.

Shame to the slothful and woe to the weak one;
   Death to the dreadful who turn to flee.
Blood to the tearing, the talon'd, the beaked one;
   Timor Mortis are We.

AT THE VAULT OF DAYBREAK

You turning world, pouring beneath our pinions,
Hoist the hoar sun to welcome morning's minions.

See, on each breast the scarlet and vermilion,
Hear, from each throat the clarion and carillion.

Hark, the wild wandering lines in black battalions,
Heaven's horns and hunters, dawn-bright hounds and stallions.

Free, free: far, far: and fair on wavering wings
Comes Anser albifrons, and sounds, and sings.

D'YE KEN WILLIAM TWYTI?

'D'ye ken William Twyti
  With his jerkin so dagged?
D'ye ken William Twyti
  Who never yet lagged?
Yes, I ken William Twyti,
  And he ought to be gagged
With his hounds and his horn in the morning.'

A DRAY HORSE

Meek Hercules – passion of arched power bowed in titanic affection,
Docile though vanquishing, stout-limber in vastness, plunging
   and spurning thy road –
Tauten thy traces, triumph past me, take thy shattering direction
Through misty Glasgow, dragging in a tremendous beer-waggon thy
   cobble-thundering load.

Thy wineskin of bright blood holds dim traits of trembling Diana –
Of the blood hunter, the quelled virgin, surging to urging thighs.
It speaks of that ground-beater in her beauty, that trampler,
   turf-disdainer,
Poised, reined, heeled, hurled to an impetuous rise.

It speaks of him also, sprig of racecourses – Satan, wild-eyed
   wild-oat-sower,
Of him the nappy scion, nerve-spun heritor of frenetic sires,
Of him, the sinew-modelled, fancy-manèd, high-stepping pace-goer,
The dandy tragedian, consumed by mental fires.

But thou, nearer than these, art bodily perfection.
Dear horse, thou art certainly the most beautiful of things.
Thou art fire-stamping Colossus: thou art thunder:
Go, Hercules, beget thy stallion kings!

IN A LOWER KEY

'And although you can write
poetry out of despair, just as you
can write it out of joy, it's very
hard to write it out of depression.'
                    – Michael Innes

Well, of course, it would have to be
In a lower key,
Not lyrical or emphatic or transported,
Simply aborted.
You could say, Why? Or, Well? Or, it is so!
Or merely, I don't know.
You could say, Why say? Or, best of all,
Say nothing at all.

THE TOWER OF SILOAM

Is it correct to sing in rhyme
Tragedy's boredom? Is it right to tell
The fatuous common side of time,
The innocent dead without crime
On whom the Tower of Siloam fell?

A million mothers weep today
Sons lost by nothing more than growth.
A million sweethearts sigh to say
'It did not happen in that way:
It fell for one – not neither – nor for both.'

There – at that Tick – with clash and shock
The twelve-year-old, his father's tender care,
Slid under the bus. And his clock
Went, between Tick and hoped-for Tock,
Mixed with a bicycle, no one knows where.

And is it wise or kind to add
To aching Sweetheart or to Dad,
They will forget, they won't be sad?
Sons do go, and it matters not a jot
Whether the Tower of Siloam fell or not.

VERSES

in aid of a PUBLIC SUBSCRIPTION
to restore the church bells of ALDERNEY
in CORONATION YEAR,
taken away by the Germans

Wind up the curling stairs
Set in the wall;
Ten, twenty, thirty, forty,
Hardly yet worn at all.

In this square, empty room,
Silently serene,
Lit from above, no view,
Is where the bells have been.

Clean as a pin,
Unstirred
By mouse or man,
Is the great box where they were heard.

They are to come back,
They are, they are,
From their long bundling
And pilgrimage of war.

They are to swoop again
And plainly must
Jollify marriages and mourn
The ancestral dust.

Deep-tongued, rehung,
Raucous and real,
They are to celebrate
Their liberation, jubilation,
coronation peal.

FLORENTINE PIGEONS

The plate armour of the Floretine pigeons!
Each gunmetal feather fitting over the one beneath!
A mineral oil should be used for them in these regions
To preserve each grey steely slide in its sheath.

Your mail it is Milanese, cap à pied to the tips –
Has its primaries, secondaries, mantles and trains,
Nothing moulted. Every plume intergrips
Like snake scales and pistons of engines of aeroplanes.

Coo-Coo and Ri-Coo you moan for the Medici,
Slanting up and down over the Latin tiles.
And the roofs are red, ramshackle, rust to see,
Old and unpredictable in their styles.

That chimney of small Roman bricks has Venetian arches,
Cracked, smoky, displastered. And those pleasure domes
Look like broken-down greenhouses shaded in khakis
And the airy acres of architecture make good homes.

There are the T.V. masts and the Pitti and the Uffizi
And Santa This and That and the deep-toned bells.
And all the Indian-red which is upside down to me
Is the terra-cotta world where the dove dwells.

Holy Ghosts? The Spring? The Annunciation?
You coo while a skewbald cat strikes with her poker face.
Italian, Roman, perhaps of the Etruscan nation,
You are high high high, wise as old, and you swirl
    like a greystorm in space.

SONG FROM 'TRISTRAM'

Wave says to wave, Why did we break, why did we come?
Grass says to green grass, Why so green?
Why the trouble of beauty, to be seen and then not to be seen?
All is as it is. Endure, be numb:
Might Have Been, Was and Is must come to be Has Been.

TO MY SELF,
FORTY YEARS AGO

Little child
Who was me once,
My pity on you –
And reverence.

Terence, if I
Could return
My drear tideway
To your bright burn,

If we could meet
Where I once strayed,
The betrayer
And the betrayed.

If we could win back
In Time's defiance,
Would you be afeared of me,
Ten-year-old Terence!

No, you would not fear.
You would love, trust,
Cherish, admire
This tedious dust.

For oh! we were all brimming once
With the sun-sparkled dew.
One heart could have loved this hulk –
The ignorant heart of you.

VODKA POEM
TO RICHARD BURTON

Richard ap Richard –
For you are
Your father and your son –
Are you the spendthrift and the spent,
The slayer slain in one?
Believer who does not believe,
Munificent and mean,
Trustless and trusting, insecure,
How will you get you clean?
Do not. But suffer. Understand.
Mascara nor the dust of coal
Nor male nor female lashes fanned
Are Gwalia, nor the whole.

FOR JULIE ANDREWS

Helen, whose face was fatal, must have wept
Many long nights alone.
And every night
Men died, she cried, and happy Paris kept
Sweet Helen.

Julie, the thousand prows aimed at her heart,
The tragic Queen, comedian and clown,
Keeps Troy together, not apart,
Nor lets one tower fall down.

AFTERWORD

In arriving at this selection of White's poetry my primary source has been the White Collection held in the Humanities Research Center at The University of Texas at Austin. As a look at the notes which follow will show, many of the poems presented here were originally written by White in his journals. Other poems, as indicated, were made the subjects of separate autograph manuscripts. There are three gatherings of poems in the White Collection: one of verse written during the years 1938-1941, and two compiled in 1961 from which his privately printed Alderney Edition was drawn. Not all of the poems which appear in White's journals prior to 1942 were included in his 1938-1941 gathering; almost all of the poems from this gathering, however, were used by White in his 1961 gatherings, and show up in the Alderney Edition. There are several poems in the Alderney Edition for which no drafts appear in the White Collection.

Other sources: the scarce *Loved Helen and Other Poems* and *Verses*, both afforded me by my friend François Gallix; White's biography by Sylvia Townsend Warner; White's published works.

In preparing each poem for publication, I have tried to take into account all versions (some poems have many drafts, some few); no poem is likely to agree in all particulars with any one of White's own versions. With one poem ('Reading Friar Clynn'), I have substituted an original version for a tar different later one ('The Silly Old Man') which White himself preferred. I have silently made changes to White's punctuation and have at times reined his exuberant spelling. Very occasionally I have supplied or transposed a word which, it seemed evident from the context, was either missing or misplaced.

K. S.

NOTES

(Poems followed by the letters AE (Alderney Edition) were included by White in his privately printed, limited edition (100 copies) of *Verses*, 1962.)

Pages 3-6. 'Paris', 'Lost', 'Cold', and 'Journey's End' appeared in *Loved Helen and Other Poems* (London: Chatto & Windus, 1929).

Page 7. 'Dr Prisonface'. In 1931 White, while teaching at a preparatory school in the south of England, sent this poem in a letter to his Cambridge tutor L. J. Potts; it appears in Sylvia Townsend Warner's *T. H. White: A Biography* (London: Jonathan Cape and Chatto & Windus, 1967; New York: The Viking Press, 1968) – hereafter referred to as Warner – on pages 54-55.

Page 9. 'Of Hapless Father'. This poem appears in White's journal entry for 1 December 1938 and is quoted in part by Warner, page 21.

Page 10. 'Looking at the Skull of St Andrew on the Altar at Amalfi'. AE. This poem is said to have been published in *The Listener*. Part of it appears in *First Lesson* (London: Chatto & Windus, 1932; New York: Alfred A. Knopf, Inc., 1933).

Page 11. 'Reading Giraldus Cambrensis'. AE. This poem appears in White's journal entry of 19 June 1940, and was published in *The Dublin Magazine* of October/December 1940 and in *The Atlantic* of December 1940.

Page 13. 'Reading Friar Clynn'. Written on stationery from Healion's Hotel, Belmullet, this poem is included in White's manuscript gathering of 'Verses, 1938-1941', and was probably composed during the last days of 1939 or the first days of 1940 when White was visiting the coast of County Mayo. A later and greatly changed version ('The Silly Old Man') is included in the Alderney Edition. A translation of the Latin is given in *The Book of Merlyn* (Austin & London: The University of Texas Press, 1977).

Page 15. 'Endurance Vile'. AE. The title of this poem was originally given to 'The Tower of Siloam', of which this poem was a continuation.

Pages 16-21. 'A Choir Boy Singing', 'Le Commun Advenement', 'All Saints' Day' (White's journal entry for 1 November 1939), 'A Joy Proposed'

(White's journal entry for 16 November 1939), 'On Falling in Love Again After Seven Years', and 'My Jack-Merlin Balan' (White's journal entry for 12 November 1939; published in *The Dublin Magazine* of April/June 1940), were all included in the Alderney Edition.

Page 22. 'Lines Cut in the Cottage Window'. This appears in White's journal entry for 18 October 1938, written while White was living in the gamekeeper's cottage on the Stowe estate.

Page 23. 'Stars and Mountains' (White's journal entry for 23 September 1939) appears in Warner, page 147.

Page 24. 'The Stuffed Pheasant'. AE. This poem appears in White's journal entry for 12 November 1939, and was published in *The Dublin Magazine* of April/June 1940. There was a stuffed pheasant in Mr and Mrs McDonagh's farmhouse, Doolistown, where White lodged 1939-1945.

Page 25. 'The Game-Keeper'. This poem was written in White's journal entry for 30 September 1939, and was published in *The Dublin Magazine* of January/March 1940.

Page 26. 'Boo to a Heron'. AE. Appearing in White's journal entry for 12 November 1939, this poem was published in *The Dublin Magazine* of April/June 1940.

Page 27. 'Curlews'. This poem was written in White's journal entry for 29 May 1942. A grove of lovely one-hundred-year-old Douglas firs, growing in a bog where White often walked in winter, was hacked down and the bog burned.

Page 29. 'The Cow'. This was written in White's journal entry for 1 November 1939.

Page 30. 'A Young Cock Grouse'. AE. White wrote this in his journal entry for 12 November 1939; it was published in *The Dublin Magazine* of April/June 1940, and is quoted in part in Warner, page 157.

Page 31. 'Letter from a Goose-Shooter'. AE. This poem, inspired by White's stay on Inniskea, is found in his journal entry for 19 December 1939, and was published by Cyril Connolly in *Horizon* in January 1942.

Page 33. 'Wild Geese'. AE. This poem is found in White's journal entry for 26 November 1939.

Pages 34 and 35. 'Sheskin' (White's journal entry for 24 September 1939; published in *The Dublin Magazine* of January/March 1940; quoted in Warner, pages 147-8) and 'Good-Bye Now' (White's journal entry for 30 September 1939; published in *The Dublin Magazine* of January/March 1940) were inspired by White's September tenancy of Sheskin Lodge, County Mayo. The holiday houseparty to which the young author had so enthusiastically invited his friends was ill-fated: on 9 September White learned that England and Germany were at war; David Garnett immediately returned to England; other guests never arrived. 'Stars and Mountains', 'Sheskin', 'Good-Bye Now', and 'When Dynasties Are Dead', with their mentions of Nephin and Slieve Car – mountains in the vicinity – were all written about Sheskin Lodge. 'Burdheachas/Le dia' is White's spelling for the Irish: 'Thanks (or gratitude) to God'.

Page 36. 'When Dynasties Are Dead'. This poem appears undated on the third page of White's journal for 1941-42.

Pages 37-40. 'Dogs Have No Souls' (White's journal entry for 12 November 1939), AE, 'Off to the Wars', AE, and 'Brownie, I Am Free of You' (White's journal entry for 25 November 1944) are concerned with White's beloved red setter, his companion for eleven years. A lock of her hair still alive and glowing adorns a page of photographs in his journal.

Pages 41-44. 'Love Is Blind', 'All for Love', 'No Trouble' (White's journal entry for 23 September 1939), and 'Detachment' (White's journal entry for 22 September 1939) are all included in the Alderney Edition.

Pages 45-52. 'These Are The Easy Verses' and 'Napoleon Crowned Himself' are both found under White's journal entry for 23 September 1939; 'Now Is A Moveable Feast', AE, 'A Train', and 'An Outmoded Sonnet', AE, under the journal entry for 25 September 1939; 'Time Fast and Time Slow', AE, under the entry for 23 October 1939; 'High Time' appears in the manuscript gathering of White's 'Verses 1939-41'; 'The Schoolmaster's Song' is the subject of a separate autograph manuscript dated 1944.

Page 53. 'Palomides to La Beale Isoud' appears in *The Witch In The Wood* (London: Collins, 1940; New York: G. P. Putnam's Sons, 1939).

Page 54. 'The Ordeal Hymn'. This poem is found in *The Sword in the Stone* (London: Collins, 1938; New York: G. P. Putnam's Sons, 1939; Time Incorporated, 1964) and in *The Once and Future King* (London: Collins, 1958; New York, G. P. Putnam's Sons, 1958).

Page 55. 'At the Vault of Daybreak'. This poem appears in *The Once and Future King* and in *The Book of Merlyn*.

Page 56. 'D'Ye Ken William Twyti?' is found in *The Sword in the Stone* and *The Once and Future King*.

Page 57. 'A Dray Horse', AE, is said to have been published in *The Listener*.

Page 58. 'In a Lower Key'. This poem is the subject of a separate undated manuscript.

Page 59. 'The Tower of Siloam'. AE.

Page 60. 'Verses in Aid of a Public Subscription'. AE.

Page 61. 'Florentine Pigeons'. This poem is found under White's journal entry for 29 January 1963, and is quoted in Warner, page 319.

Page 62. 'Song from *Tristram*'. AE. In 1958 the BBC suggested to White that he write a play for them; White began work on a play about Tristram and Mark. Though he subsequently thought of the project as a book ('The Sad One'), and sent notes on it to Julie Andrews and Richard Burton, he abandoned the undertaking.

Page 63. Early versions of 'To My Self, Forty Years Ago', AE, appear in the endpapers of White's copy of Walter de la Mare's *Stories, Essays and Poems* and in White's journal entry for 17 November 1940.

Page 64. 'Vodka Song for Richard Burton'. AE. 'Gwalia' may be the Welsh 'Gwala', meaning 'sufficiency' or 'enough'. White's spelling is notoriously unpredictable.

Page 65. 'To Julie Andrews'. AE. Richard Burton and Julie Andrews were, of course, the stars of *Camelot*, the musical made from *The Once and Future King*; White, who attended the tryouts of the play, developed a great friendship for both its stars, and was particularly fond of Miss Andrews who, with her husband, visited White on Alderney.